2, 4, Skip Count SOME MORE

by Thomas K. and Heather Adamson

Consultant:
Tamara Olson, Associate Professor
Department of Mathematical Sciences
Michigan Technological University

CAPSTONE PRESS
a capstone imprint

A+ Books are published by Capstone Press,
1710 Roe Crest Drive, North Mankato, Minnesota 56003.
www.capstonepub.com

Books published by Capstone Press are manufactured with paper
containing at least 10 percent post-consumer waste.

Library of Congress Cataloging-in-Publication Data

Cataloging-in-publication information is on file with the Library of Congress.
ISBN 978-1-4296-7707-3 (hardcover)
ISBN 978-1-4296-7856-8 (paperback)

Credits

Kristen Mohn, editor; Gene Bentdahl, designer; Svetlana Zhurkin, media researcher; Laura Manthe,
production specialist; Sarah Schuette, photo stylist; Marcy Morin, studio scheduler

Photo Credits

All photos by Capstone Studio/Karon Dubke except: Alamy/Juniors Bildarchiv, cover;
iStockphoto/kali9, 24–25; Shutterstock/James M. Phelps, Jr., 1

Note to Parents, Teachers, and Librarians

This Fun with Numbers book uses photos of everyday objects in a nonfiction format to introduce
the concept of skip counting, including counting by twos, threes, fours, fives, and tens. *2, 4, Skip
Count Some More* is designed to be read aloud to a pre-reader or to be read independently by
an early reader. The book encourages further learning by including the following sections: Table
of Contents, Taking It Further, Read More, and Internet Sites. Early readers may need assistance
using these features.

Printed in the United States of America in North Mankato, Minnesota.
102011   006405CGS12

TABLE of CONTENTS

What Is Skip Counting?

Lunchtime! We're making four sandwiches. How many slices of bread will we need?

Skip counting is a fast way to find out.

Instead of counting each number, you "skip" over one or more numbers according to a pattern. You can skip count by groups of two or more.

Each sandwich has two slices of bread.
Let's skip count by twos to get the total.

2

4

6

8

How many hands? We could count them one by one, but it's faster to skip count. Each person has two hands.

What if we want to count fingers? Counting by ones could take awhile. Each hand has five fingers.

15

20

10

25

5

30

That's 40 fingers waiting for their sandwiches!

35

40

Counting Pairs

Let's count the shoes in the shoe cubby at Funland.

Shoes come in pairs. A pair is two. There are 10 pairs in the cubby. That's 10 kids playing in socks!

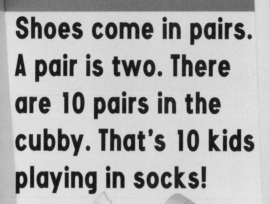

Count by twos to find out how many shoes there are.

Even numbers, such as 20, can be put into groups of two with none left over. Odd numbers always have one left over without a partner.

There are 10 kids with 20 feet and 20 shoes.
That's even. But only 19 feet have socks.
That's odd!

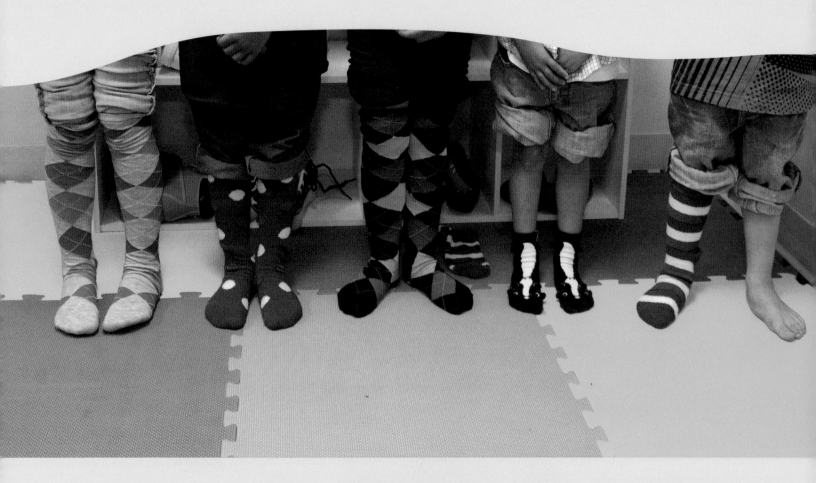

Where's your other sock, Darren?

Skip Counting Money

The penny jar is getting full. Let's count them. No, let's skip count them!

Ella stacks the pennies in groups of 10. Skip count by 10s to count the pennies. Ten stacks make 100 pennies. That equals one dollar!

Who put these four nickels in the penny jar?
A nickel is five cents. Skip count by fives to
find out how much the nickels add up to.

Solving Problems

Help Shawn fix the gap in his wall. Count the bumps in the missing section. There are eight bumps. How many of this green brick would you need to get to eight? It has two bumps. Skip count by twos: 2, 4, 6, 8. That's four of these little bricks.

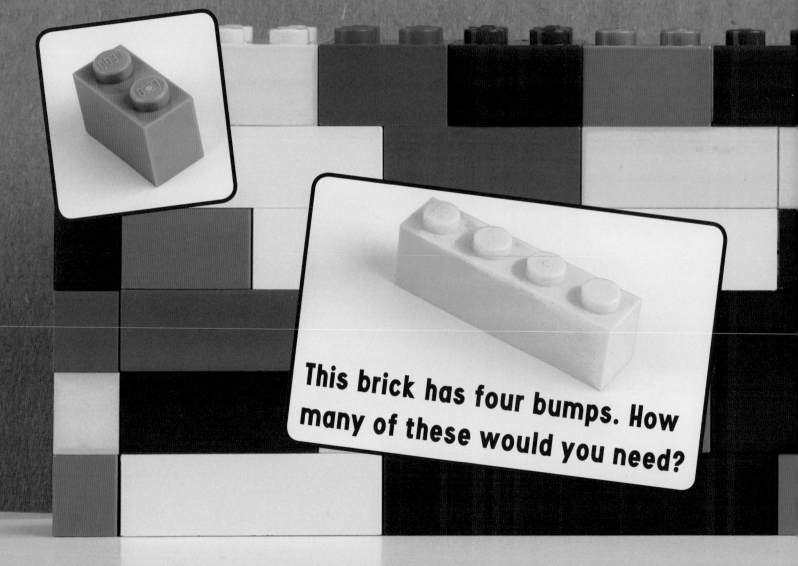

This brick has four bumps. How many of these would you need?

Can you find one brick that would fill the spot by itself?

Who's hungry? There are two packages of hot dog buns. Each row has four buns. That's 4, 8, 12, 16 buns.

The hot dog package has two rows of five dogs. Skip count by fives: 5, 10 hot dogs. Will two packages of buns be enough for one package of hot dogs?

This picture graph shows which ice cream flavor the second grade likes best.

There are two strawberry scoops, three vanilla scoops, and five chocolate scoops. That's 10 scoops, but there are more than 10 kids in second grade.

= 3 kids

The graph saves space by making each scoop stand for three people. Skip counting by threes will give us the real numbers. Skip count the chocolate scoops: 3, 6, 9, 12, 15. Fifteen kids picked chocolate as their favorite.

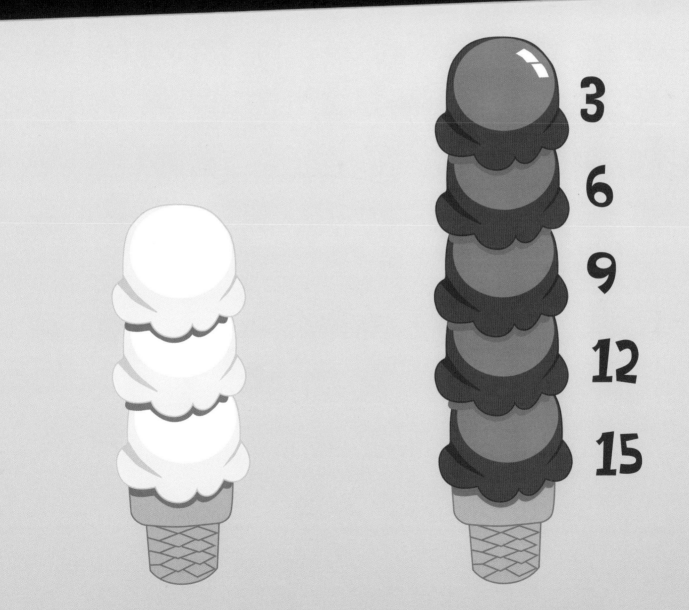

3
6
9
12
15

Skip count all the scoops to find the total children in second grade. How many are there?

These carpet squares are lined up nice and neat. To find out how many kids are coming to story time, we can skip count them. The squares are lined up in four rows of four. Skip count by fours: 4, 8, 12, 16 kids.

Here they come!

Clocks and Skip Counting

Clocks make us skip count. The long minute hand counts five minutes between each big number.

If the minute hand is on the 1, it is five minutes past the hour.

If the minute hand is on the 2, it is 10 minutes past.

When the minute hand points straight down at the 6, we say it is "half past the hour." Count by fives to find out how many minutes half past is.

Forward or Backward

You can even skip count backward! The ticket seller skip counts backward as she sells tickets. Each seat holds two riders, so she counts backward by twos.

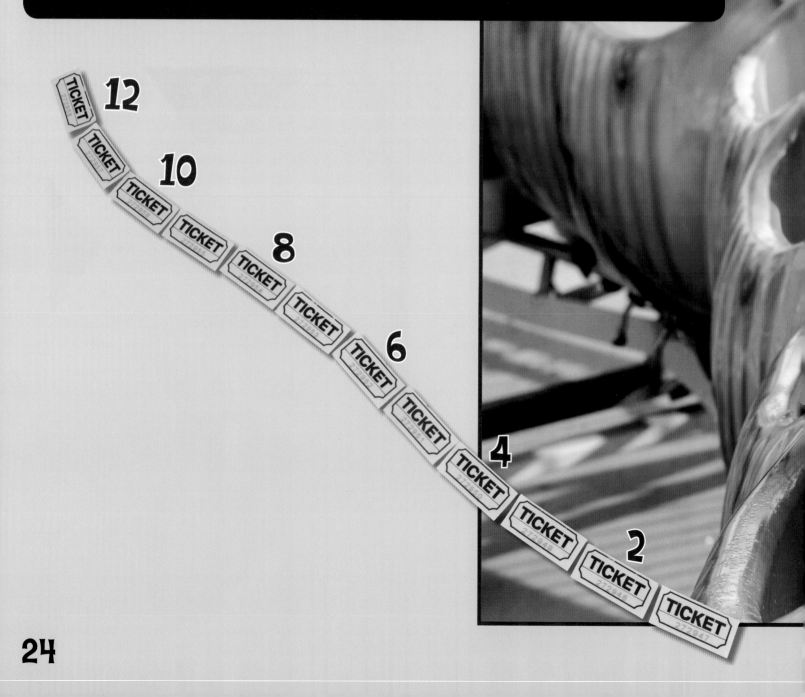

12
10
8
6
4
2

The ride holds 12 riders. She sells two tickets. Ten seats left. She sells two more. Eight seats left. She keeps selling: 6, 4, 2, 0. All aboard!

These piles are set up for skip counting. Can you tell what the skip is?

Something is wrong with these bug skip count groups. What is it?

How would you skip count these cupcakes?

Skip counting helps you count in a snap. 2, 4, 6, 8, what do we appreciate? Skip counting!

CHECK YOUR SKIP COUNTS

Pages 8-9:
2, 4, 6, 8, 10, 12, 14, 16, 18, 20. Ten children have 20 shoes!

Page 13:
5, 10, 15, 20. Four nickels equal 20 cents.

Page 14:
You would need two of the yellow bricks.

Page 15:
The blue brick has eight bumps. That will fill the gap.

Pages 16-17:
Sixteen hot dog buns will be enough for 10 hot dogs. There will be six buns left over.

Pages 18-19:
If each scoop equals three children, that's 3, 6, 9, 12, 15, 18, 21, 24, 27, 30 children in second grade. Counting by threes takes practice!

Page 23:
Skip count by fives to get to half past the hour: 5, 10, 15, 20, 25, 30. A half-hour is 30 minutes.

Page 26:
The third group of bugs has only three instead of four. You can't skip count if the groups aren't the same.

Page 29:
There are five rows of five cupcakes each. That's 5, 10, 15, 20, 25 cupcakes. Yum!

TAKING IT FURTHER

Four quarters make one dollar. Skip count by fours to find out how many quarters you would need to make five dollars.

Look at the children's feet on pages 10 and 11. How would you find out how many toes are under all those socks?

In football a team can score seven points with a touchdown. Skip count by sevens to find out how many points five touchdowns are worth:

7   14   21   28   35

Now imagine your team is behind by 21 points. How many touchdowns do you need to score to catch up?

GLOSSARY

equal—being the same in amount

even—possible to divide by two

odd—not able to divide by two evenly

pair—a set of two things that make one unit

pattern—a repeating arrangement

READ MORE

Aboff, Marcie. *If You Were an Even Number.* Math Fun. Minneapolis, Minn.: Picture Window Books, 2009.

Harris, Trudy. *Splitting the Herd: A Corral of Odds and Evens.* Minneapolis, Minn.: Millbrook Press, 2008.

Murphy, Stuart J. *Spunky Monkeys on Parade.* MathStart. New York: HarperCollins Publishers, 1999.

INTERNET SITES

FactHound offers a safe, fun way to find Internet sites related to this book. All of the sites on FactHound have been researched by our staff.

Here's all you do:

Visit *www.facthound.com*

Type in this code: 9781429677073

Super-cool stuff! Check out projects, games and lots more at **www.capstonekids.com**

YEADON PUBLIC LIBRARY
809 LONGACRE BLVD.
YEADON, PA 19050
(610) 623-4090